Presidents' Day

By David F. Marx

Consultants
Nanci R. Vargus, Ed.D.
Primary Multiage Teacher
Decatur Township Schools, Indianapolis, Indiana

Katharine A. Kane, Reading Specialist
Former Language Arts Coordinator,
San Diego County Office of Education

Children's Press®
A Division of Scholastic Inc.
New York   Toronto   London   Auckland   Sydney
Mexico City   New Delhi   Hong Kong
Danbury, Connecticut

Designer: Herman Adler Design
Photo Researcher: Caroline Anderson
The image on the cover shows Abraham Lincoln on the left and
George Washington on the right.

Library of Congress Cataloging-in-Publication Data

Marx, David F.
    Presidents' Day / by David F. Marx.
       p. cm. — (Rookie read-about holidays)
    Includes index.
    Summary: Discusses the holiday known as Presidents' Day and the
significant achievements of those presidents whom it honors, George
Washington and Abraham Lincoln.
    ISBN 0-516-22268-6 (lib. bdg.)   0-516-27376-0 (pbk.)
    1. Presidents' Day—Juvenile literature. 2. Presidents—United States—
History—Juvenile literature. [1. Presidents' Day. 2. Washington, George,
1732-1799. 3. Lincoln, Abraham, 1809-1865. 4. Presidents. 5. Holidays.]
I. Title. II. Series.
E176.8.M19   2002
394.261—dc21

                                     2001002682

CHILDREN'S PRESS, and ROOKIE READ-ABOUT®,
and associated logos are trademarks and or registered trademarks
of Scholastic Library Publishing. SCHOLASTIC and associated logos
are trademarks and or registered trademarks of Scholastic Inc.
8 9 10 11 12 13 14 15 16 17 R 14 13 12 11 10 09 08 07 06 05

The United States of
America has had more
than forty presidents.

On Presidents' Day
we remember George
Washington and
Abraham Lincoln.

George Washington

They were brave and honest men. They both were leaders during times of war.

Abraham Lincoln

Long ago, there were holidays on both men's birthdays.

Lincoln's Birthday was celebrated on February 12.

Washington's Birthday was celebrated on February 22.

February

Sunday	Monday	Tuesday	Wednesday	Thursday	Friday	Saturday
				1	2	3
4	5	6	7	8	9	10
11	**Lincoln's 12 Birthday**	13	14	15	16	17
18	19	20	21	**Washington's 22 Birthday**	23	24
25	26	27	28			

Today, we celebrate both presidents' birthdays as one holiday—Presidents' Day.

February 2006

Sunday	Monday	Tuesday	Wednesday	Thursday	Friday	Saturday
			1	2	3	4
5	6	7	8	9	10	11
12	13	14	15	16	17	18
19	**20**	21	22	23	24	25
26	27	28				

It comes on the third Monday in February.

Before he was president, George Washington was a leader of the American army. He led soldiers during the Revolutionary War.

In that war, Americans fought Great Britain. Great Britain was a country that ruled America.

George Washington helped America win its freedom from Great Britain.

13

14

Washington became
the first president of the
United States in 1789.
He was president for
eight years.

Washington helped plan
the nation's new capital
city. The capital is where
the nation's leaders work.

17

When the capital city
was built, it was named
after George Washington.

Today, the president
and other United States
leaders live and work
in Washington, D.C.

Abraham Lincoln became president in 1861. He led the United States throughout the Civil War.

In this war, Americans did not fight another country. The northern states fought the southern states.

21

People in the southern states
wanted to be able to own
slaves to work on their farms.

President Lincoln wanted
to end slavery in the South.
This made the South want
to separate from the North.

President Lincoln wanted
the country to stay together.

In 1861, the North started
to fight the South. President
Lincoln led the northern
states during the war.

After four years of fighting,
the North won.

President Lincoln was once again the leader of both the North and the South. He was able to reunite our country and he set the slaves free.

Leading a nation through war is never easy. Making the right choices as president is not always easy.

Presidents Washington and Lincoln tried to do what was right...not just what was easy.

29

Words You Know

Abraham Lincoln

Civil War

George Washington

Revolutionary War

30

slaves

Washington, D.C.

Index

About the Author

David F. Marx is an author and editor of children's books. He resides in the Chicago area.

Photo Credits